What to do
when your mom or dad says . . .
"STAND UP STRAIGHT!"

By
JOY WILT BERRY

Living Skills Press
Fallbrook, California

Distributed by:

Word, Incorporated
4800 W. Waco Drive
Waco, TX 76710

Copyright ©1983 Joy Wilt Berry
Printed in the United States of America.
Library of Congress Catalog Card Number: 83-080-843
ISBN 0-941510-19-0

Dear Parents,

"STAND UP STRAIGHT!" You've probably said that more than once to your children. Most likely it was because they were slouching over and looking dreadful in the process. Bad posture looks terrible on anyone, but more important than how it looks is how it affects one's body. Bad posture can keep a person's body from functioning properly. This is because it stifles normal physical responses by hindering the work of the central nervous system. The spinal column is one of the main components of the central nervous system. It can do its job only if it is held in a correct position. Good posture holds the spinal column in a correct position.

Thus, good posture is essential for good looks *and* for good health.

Let's talk about how you can help your children improve their posture.

First, your children must be made aware of the fact that good posture is vital to looking good and feeling well. Then they must be taught what good posture is and exactly how to achieve it.

This book can help your children learn these things. It will tell them good posture is necessary; then it will define good posture and carefully explain how it can be maintained.

To get the most out of this book, I recommend that you go through it with your children, encouraging them to apply each concept and illustration to their own bodies. After you have shared this book with your children, give it to them to use as a resource whenever they need it.

3

The time you spend doing these things will benefit both you and your children. For one thing, helping your children with their posture may motivate you to improve your own. But more important than this is the positive effect your efforts will have on your relationship with your children.

Because "an ounce of education is worth a pound of nagging," you'll find that the time you spend helping your children develop good posture will minimize the time you spend nagging at them to **"STAND UP STRAIGHT!"**

Sincerely,

Joy Wilt Berry

Has you mother or father ever told you to...

STAND UP STRAIGHT!

Whenever you are told to stand up straight, do
you wonder. . .

If any of this sounds familiar to you, you are going to **love** this book!

Because it will tell you why you should stand up straight and exactly how you should do it.

Standing up straight (maintaining good posture) makes you look better.

Which do you think looks better?

Good posture also helps your body to work right, and thus it makes you feel better.

GOOD POSTURE WHILE STANDING

To maintain good posture while you are standing, remember these things:

CORRECT INCORRECT INCORRECT

- Make sure that your head is erect with your chin parallel to the floor. Don't carry your head too far back or too far forward.

• Your shoulders should be relaxed, but not
hunched.

• Your chest should be raised, not fallen in.

- Your back should be straight, not curved in or out.

• Your abdomen (stomach) should be in, not out.

CORRECT   INCORRECT

- Your buttocks (bottom) should be in, not out.

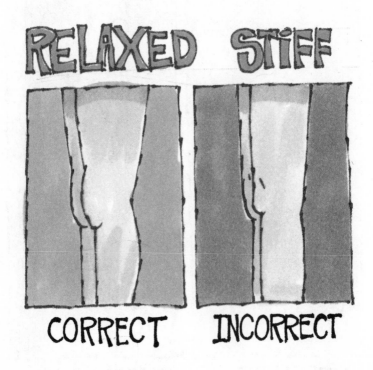

RELAXED **STIFF**

CORRECT **INCORRECT**

- Your knees should be straight but comfortably relaxed, rather than stiff.

CORRECT   INCORRECT

HE LOOKS AS IF HE'S POSING FOR A FASHION MAGAZINE.

- Your weight should be balanced on both feet.

When your posture is good, these parts of your body are in line:

- your earlobe
- the tip of your shoulder
- the middle of your hip
- the middle of your knee
- your front anklebone

When your posture is good, your head will line up with your feet.

To get your body lined up properly, pretend that you are being pulled up by the hair on the top of your head, and tense or tuck your buttocks in and under as tightly as you can.

If you do this, everything else will line itself up naturally.

GOOD POSTURE WHILE MOVING

When you are moving, it's important to keep your back straight.

When you lean forward or reach for something,
lean from your hips.

When you are working at a desk, lean forward from your hips.

It's also important that you keep flexible when you are moving. Don't be too rigid.

GOOD POSTURE WHILE WALKING

To maintain good posture while walking, do these things:

- Point your feet straight ahead (or very slightly outward if that's more comfortable for you), rather than to either side.

FEET POINTING STRAIGHT

CORRECT   INCORRECT

- Put one foot directly in front of the other.

25

RIGHT ARM BACK

LEFT ARM FORWARD

THIS IS TOO COMPLICATED FOR ME!

RIGHT FOOT FORWARD

- When your right foot is forward, your left arm should be forward and your right arm back. When your left foot is forward, your right arm should be forward and your left arm back.

- Swing your arms from your shoulders with your elbows close to your body but not tense. Keep your arms relaxed and try not to bend your elbows as your arms come forward.

- Try not to shuffle.

• Try not to walk heavily.

GOOD POSTURE WHILE CLIMBING STAIRS

To maintain good posture whenever you go up or down stairs, do these things:

- Keep your knees flexed. Don't bend and straighten them as you climb stairs. Your large thigh muscles should be doing the work.

- Place your entire foot on each step. If the steps are too narrow to allow for this, turn both of your feet in the same direction.

- Keep your head erect. Look with your eyes, not with your head.

• If there is a handrail, use it.

GOOD POSTURE WHILE MOVING, LIFTING AND CARRYING HEAVY OBJECTS

When moving something, keep your back straight, bend at the hips, and let your arms and legs do all of the pushing and pulling.

CORRECT   INCORRECT

Also let your arms and legs do the work when you are carrying something. Keep your back straight, and hold heavy objects as close to you as possible.

When you must lift something, do these things:

BACK STRAIGHT

KNEES BENT

Step 1

Squat down next to the object by bending your knees. Keep your back straight.

Step 2

Get as close as you can to the object by bending forward at the hips, not at the waist. Again, keep your back straight.

Step 3

Get hold of the object by putting your arms around it or your hands under it.

Step 4

Bend back at the hips and stand up by straightening your knees. Remember to keep the object close to you while you are lifting or carrying it.

GOOD POSTURE WHILE SITTING

EDGE OF CHAIR

To maintain good posture while sitting down, turn until your back is to the chair and you can feel the edge of the seat with the backs of your legs.

Slide one foot slightly back under the chair and, with your back straight, lower yourself into the chair. Use your knees and thighs, not the upper part of your body.

To sit in a chair correctly, maintain good posture and place the small of your back against the back of the chair.

CORRECT   INCORRECT

Put your hands in a comfortable position in your lap or on the arms of the chair. Keep your feet flat on the floor or cross your legs at the ankle.

When you get up, put your feet close under your
body, with one foot in front of the other.

Push up with your rear foot and straighten your
legs.

Exercises strengthen the muscles that can help you maintain good posture. Here are some exercises to improve your posture:

Exercise 1 — Lateral Bending

Stand erect with arms hanging naturally at sides. Bend slowly to one side beginning with the head, neck, shoulders, chest and lower back, allowing arm to descend naturally with the bend (exercise should not involve the hips). Then return trunk to the starting position in the reverse order. Repeat five times on each side.

Exercise 2 — Rocking Chin Tuck

Sit erect. Turn head as far to one side as possible.
Then raise it (as if looking at the ceiling) and rock
it down to touch chin on the shoulder. This
nodding motion is repeated five times. Return the
head to its normal position. Repeat exercise on the
opposite side. The entire exercise should be done
five times.

Exercise 3 — Trunk Slump and Return

Sit in a straight chair. Bend the trunk forward as if to place the head between the knees, effecting the motion in the spinal column rather than in the hips. Return the body to its starting position, beginning the movement with the lower segments and proceeding to the upper segments (until you feel as "tall" as possible). Repeat 10 times.

Exercise 4 — Hyperextension

Lie face down to the floor, arms extended out to the sides. Raise arms, head and shoulders (chest) from prone position by contracting back muscles (usual height of chin from floor: 20 inches). After holding this position a short period, slowly return to starting position. Relax. Repeat exercise five times.

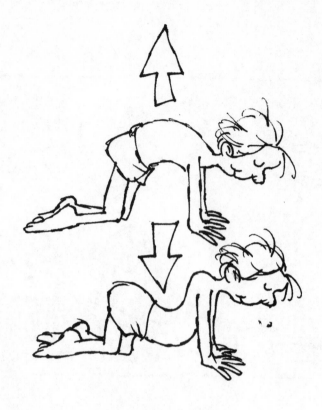

Exercise 5 — Arch and Sway

Assume a position on "all fours" (hands and knees) with arms and thighs in vertical position from shoulders and hips, respectively. Roll pelvis, arching back upward and lowering head, trying to round spine as much as possible. Hold this position briefly. Then allow pelvis to rock in opposite direction, allowing spine to sway or sag and tilting head upward. Maintain this position briefly. Relax, then return to arched position. Repeat ten times.

Exercise 6 — Rock and Roll

Lie on back. Flex knees upward to chest and retain this position by holding knees firmly with hands and arms. Roll backward toward shoulders, flexing spine to its maximum. Hold position briefly, then roll back to starting position. Repeat, allowing gravity and body weight to force the spine to flex. Repeat ten times.

THE END of having to be told to stand up straight!

48